Building Bridges
to the Heart of the Community
SIX STEPS TO CREATING A PARISH COVENANT

Stephanie Moore and Leisa Anslinger

CATHOLIC
LIFE & FAITH

ACKNOWLEDGEMENTS

We wish to express our deep and sincere gratitude to the many pastors, staff members, and parishioners who, through their leadership, vision and dedication, continue to build on the research and experience captured in these workbooks. A special thank you for the specific and ongoing support of Monsignor Bill Hanson, Fr. James Coyne, Fr. James Mallon, and Fr. Chris Heath.

We particularly wish to give special recognition to Fr. Ron Schmit, pastor at St. Anne Parish, Byron, CA and Fr. Jan Schmidt, former pastor at Immaculate Heart of Mary, who, along with their staff and parishioner leaders, developed specific covenant processes and examples that are highlighted in this workbook.

DUPLICATION POLICY AND INFORMATION

This document contains extensive study and years of experience of the authors and draws on published research of numerous organizations. It is for the guidance of your organization only. Worksheets may be reproduced for your use; masters of the worksheets are made available through the link provided in this workbook. No changes may be made to this document without the express written permission of Catholic Life and Faith.

Building Bridges to the Heart of the Community © 2015 Catholic Life and Faith

BUILDING BRIDGES TO THE HEART OF THE COMMUNITY
Six Steps to Creating a Parish Covenant

FROM THE HEART OF A PASTOR

Someone once said "God is more verb than a noun." I believe that this is the way a true disciple thinks about her or his relationship with the Risen Lord. As a noun it is too tempting to think of God as something or someone separate and removed from ourselves. However, as a verb we conceive of God as an active energy working in and through us—creating, nurturing, sustaining, healing, forgiving, calling us together and transforming us.

The Parish Covenant is one important way that disciples can identify and articulate the movement of the Holy Spirit of God in our individual lives and our parish community. What we have identified at St Anne as the elements of our Covenant to "Worship, Connect, Grow and Serve" are bridges that we are invited to cross as 'servant-disciple-apostles of God's mercy.'

In his Bull of Indiction for the Jubilee Year of Mercy, Pope Francis states that mercy is "the bridge that connects God and man, opening our hearts to the hope of being loved forever despite our sinfulness." The Parish Covenant is the invitation to cross that bridge.

— Fr. Ron Schmit, Pastor, St. Anne Church, Byron, California

INTRODUCTION

What are your greatest hopes for your parish and its people? Do you look around and think "it could be so much better if more people were really engaged here"? Are parishioners committed to Christ and to the parish, or do they just seem to come and go, without living and growing in faith? How can you build bridges to the heart of the community, and through the community to Christ?

Helping people deepen their relationship with Jesus Christ and live as Christian disciples is every parish's primary goal and mission. The Church exists to evangelize.[1] We know that the real desire of many parishioners is to fall in love with God and to live their faith as Christians in their daily lives. These parishioners come to Mass every Sunday, are deeply rooted in the faith community, and carry the presence of Christ with them in their interactions with others. These parishioners are engaged in the parish and their relationship with Christ grows as a result. Many others stay on the edges of parish life, however. They are not engaged in the parish community and consequently do not live or grow in faith as deeply as they might.

The impact is not only on the people who are already part of your parish. Consciously or unconsciously, when people walk through your parish doors, they quickly assess whether or not your parish can have a place in their lives. They need to feel welcome and valued, and have an immediate sense that the parish is a place where they can belong in order for them to open their minds and hearts to God. They may not consciously think about it, but intuitively know that the process of becoming a member of a parish is about forming a relationship with the community and its people.

As we shared in the first workbook of the Bridges Leadership Series, "Building Bridges to the Heart of Discipleship," there are three bridges that are foundational to helping people develop an initial and ongoing relationship with the parish and through

---

[1] Evangelii Nuntiandi, 14

the parish, with Christ: Welcome, Friendship and Sharing. *But that is only a beginning!* Significant research also shows that in order to create an culture in which the majority of parishioners participate fully in the life of the parish, people need to understand what their parish offers that will lead to their spiritual growth and deepening relationship with God. It is important that the parish clearly articulates the expectation it has for each individual to fully participate in the life of the parish. The parish also must help parishioners understand the meaning and impact of such full participation in order for the parish to grow as an engaging and evangelizing community.[2]

St. John Paul II captured this when he said, "To make the Church the home and school of communion: that is the great challenge facing us…if we wish to be faithful to God's plan and respond to the world's deepest yearnings."[3] The more we become engaged in the parish, the more we grow in communion with Christ and with one another.

The average "not engaged" parishioners who remain on the periphery of the parish do not recognize the potential impact of the parish in their lives. They do not consider what their parish offers or "promises" in the way of spiritual support. Perhaps more importantly, they do not fully participate in the parish. They may hear the occasional announcement at Mass or read a notice in the bulletin, but they fail to take the invitation to heart. As a result, their weak connection with the faith community results in weakened faith.

Taking all of this into consideration, many parishes have established a parish covenant that helps to identify the "Promises" that the parish makes to its faith community in addition to the "Commitments" it asks its parishioners to make. Done well, the process of creating and introducing a covenant can have a profound impact on parishioners, creating a parish culture in which people are regularly encouraged to make a commitment to Christ and to the parish community. A parish covenant creates a clear sense of what it means to belong to the parish and to fully participate in its overall mis-

---

[2] Winseman, Albert L., *Growing an Engaged Church*, New York, Gallup Press, 2006, 84-85

[3] *Novo Millennio Ineunte*, 43

sion, for current parishioners and those who come to experience the parish for the first time. Response to this covenant process has been overwhelmingly positive. The comment of new and enthusiastic parishioner at one parish captures the feelings of most: "This is the first parish I've been to that had a parish covenant. It's so nice to know all that is offered and what the expectations are!" The parish covenant is a bridge to the heart of the community, through which people come to live more deeply as Christian people, within the parish and in all of the aspects of their lives.

Our goal in this workbook is to give you a process through which you can create your own unique parish covenant. We will break down the process into six practical steps. We will explain each step and give you the tools to work through each of the steps that will guide you along the way. We will provide a solid theological foundation for the covenant. In addition, we will share the ways a covenant can be part of an already-existing stewardship commitment and renewal process. We will do all of this through an abiding recognition of the role of parish leaders in forming a community through which people are formed as missionary disciples and as good and faithful stewards.

MAKING THE MOST OF THE MATERIALS

The Bridges series has been developed for all parish leaders (formal and informal).

- ❖ Read this book in the company of others – Identify your core team that will drive the development and implementation of the covenant. This may be a newly recreated leadership group; a sub-group of your Pastoral Council or it may fall within a Stewardship Committee.

- ❖ Use the included worksheets to aid your discussion while reading.

- ❖ Take time to read and discuss together using the worksheets indicated. This will insure that your study and discussions will bear fruit in your parish community.

- ❖ Access the online worksheet materials and introductory video via the link which is included at the end of this workbook on page 85.

LEARNING VIDEO AND GUIDE

The accompanying learning video and guide is found here at the link on page 84 of this book.

The materials include:

1. A learning video which introduces the theological foundation for the covenant
2. A participant guide that accompanies this workbook and includes all worksheet masters
3. An optional introduction to engagement video
4. A study guide for Growing an Engaged Church

THE BRIDGES PROCESS: EXPLORE, SHARE AND PLAN WITH OTHERS

This workbook series is part of a larger initiative for pastoral leader development, which can be found at www.Bridge2Faith.net. You may contact us there for live events, participate in virtual gatherings, access previous session recordings, and learn about new resources as they become available. We hope you will go to the Bridges site often and stay in touch as we learn and grow together in order to build more engaging and evangelizing communities.

For whom has Bridges been developed? This series is for anyone who has influence in touching the lives of all within the parish and all who seek Christ:

- Those who have direct influence and accountability for shaping parish life, including the pastor, the staff, the Pastoral Council, and various committees/commissions (Stewardship, Finance, Evangelization, Faith Formation).

- All who form people in and teach our Catholic faith (children's catechists, RCIA team members, adult faith formation catechists and leaders).

- Those who lead ministries and organizations (Lectors, EMHC, Greeters, Hospitality, Choir, etc), as well as those who influence youth and young adult ministry.

- Any individual who is seeking ways to become more involved in shaping the direction of their parish would find this book helpful.

Our tone is intentionally informal, at times conversational. We hope you will think of us as partners in a dialogue that will lead to the development of thought and practice to strengthen your parish, forming a more engaging and evangelizing community of faith.

WHY BRIDGES?

We find the metaphor of a bridge helpful when thinking about the ways in which we can form engaging and evangelizing communities. There is nothing more precious than our relationship with Jesus Christ. And there is no one who can share our faith in quite the same way as each of us can. This is the foundation of Bridges: as members of Christ's body, parishes and people can have lasting impact on one another. We can touch those who are not rooted in a faith community, and we send one another out in mission, serving in our towns, cities, and world in Jesus' name. This gets to the heart of all we are and are called to be, as it leads us to the heart of Christ.

Why Bridges? Bridges lead us from here to there, across obstacles, through varying terrain, over tricky intersections. When we build bridges in our parishes and among our people, we stay focused on things that will lead to living faith as a disciple of Jesus Christ and a strong sense of mission. Through Bridges, we will help you develop this compelling vision for yourself as an individual and for your parish, and the skills to carry that vision out now and for the future.

Are you ready to build bridges to the heart of the community? Let's get started!

Why:
Clarifying Expectations is KEY

Why: CLARIFYING EXPECTATIONS IS KEY

"Perhaps it is surprising, or perhaps it is not, that many of you on the survey we all took a few months ago said you are not quite sure what is expected of you here. So let me tell you." This is the way one pastor began to talk with his people about expectations following their participation in the Gallup ME25 survey.[4] What is expected of people in your parish? Could the majority of parishioners name the expectations? At a time when people are shunning organized religion in great numbers, do we risk driving people away with talk of expectations? Why is this important at all?

When Growing an Engaged Church was first published in 2006, it seemed every parish leader with whom we spoke was surprised that at the foundation of the engagement process is the statement, "As a member of my congregation/parish, I know what is expected of me."[5] Parish leaders discussed this in workshops and in parish meetings. Pastors worried that talking about expectations would turn people off, and away. What they found was quite the opposite: person after person, in parish after parish, thanked the pastor and parish leadership for helping them understand what is expected of parishioners. That is what happened to the pastor whose comments were shared above. People want to know what is expected of them!

When we clarify expectations, we provide the means by which people may become part of the parish to a much greater degree. This may seem counterintuitive at

_____

[4] A link to the Gallup Faith Practice site and downloadable information on the ME25 is included on the included resource page. The link is found on page __ of this workbook.

[5] Growing an Engaged Church, 83-85

first, until we realize that every relationship has fundamental and foundational expectations. Expectations are found in all relationships. When a couple is married, for example, they make commitments to one another. There is an expectation that they will fulfill those commitments to love and honor them "in good times and in bad, in sickness and in health, all the days" of their lives. Children expect that parents will provide love, shelter, clothing and food; parents likewise expect that their children will love them, learn from them, and honor them throughout their lives, to the point of caring for them in advanced age. While often unconscious, none of these expectations can be assumed or taken for granted, and in fact, we must acknowledge that they exist in order for relationships to be healthy. Each of us could probably point to examples of times when such expectations were not met which led to an erosion of a relationship. Hopefully, we can also think of many examples in which such expectations were honored and met, often sacrificially, contributing to a life of love for the parties concerned.

Deepening belonging within the parish calls us to develop a relationship of love for one another as members of Christ's body. This relationship is often implied when people fill out registration forms or attend Mass regularly at their neighborhood parish. Clarifying expectations "raises the bar," to be certain. Yet stating the expectations for parishioners helps them understand what belonging to the parish means, and that this relationship is not only for a few "insiders" but for all parishioners — every person is of value; everyone's contributions are important. By clarifying expectations, we invite all parishioners into a relationship with one another. Through this relationship in community, we draw one another into communion with Christ.

THE BOTTOM LINE

This is the bottom line: the first and greatest expectation we may have for one another is that every person in the parish is on a journey of discipleship as a follower of Jesus Christ. Everything we are and do leads to this and flows from it. When we build bridges to the heart of the community, we build bridges to the heart of Christ who is our life, salvation, and way.

> "God has found a way to unite himself to every human being in every age. He has chosen to call them together as a people and not as isolated individuals...this people which God has chosen and called is the Church."
> The Joy of the Gospel, 113

There is something else we must acknowledge here: the expectations to which we refer are not about belief. We are speaking of expectations that build belonging. The two are distinct yet related. It could be said that we sometimes send a message that "when you believe fully enough you will belong." Yet, we learn from the engagement research that "belonging is far more likely to lead to believing."[6] Yet the engagement research and pastoral experience help us to see that when people are rooted in the good soil of the parish, they are more likely to be open to the depths of God's love and the richness of all that is within our Catholic teaching and tradition. Creating an environment in which parishioners know what it means to belong to the parish establishes a culture in which people are open to the renewed personal encounter with Jesus Christ of which Pope Francis speaks in the opening of The Joy of the

---

[6] Growing an Engaged Church, 44

Gospel.[7] From this on-going encounter with Christ, people develop an appreciation for all that we believe as Catholics. "The Church's closeness to Jesus is part of a common journey; 'communion and mission are profoundly interconnected.'"[8]

In this way, we could say that expectations that create belonging build the foundation upon which believing will be acquired or will grow. Those who already assent to the beliefs of our Catholic faith will be strengthened in their relationship with Christ and the way they live their faith through this engagement within the parish. Those who struggle with some of the tenets of Catholic teaching will be drawn to a relationship with Christ and the Church through deep belonging within the parish community.

Pope Francis inspires us with this profound message: He asks parishes to keep the physical doors of their church open, and then says, "The Church is called to be the house of the Father, with doors always wide open. One concrete sign of such openness is that our church doors should always be open, so that if someone, moved by the Spirit, comes there looking for God, he or she will not find a closed door. There are other doors that should not be closed either. Everyone can share in some way in the life of the Church; everyone can be part of the community."[9] By clarifying expectations, we create a parish culture in which many doors will be opened, through increased commitment and participation and by parishioners who come to see themselves as bridge builders

_____

[7] Pope Francis, Evangelii Gaudium." Vatican: The Holy See. Libreria Editrice Vaticana, 2013, 3

[8] Ibid, 23

[9] Ibid. 47

to the people around them. Their relationship with Christ will be strengthened, and the parish will be strengthened as a community of faith.

There is more to building an engaging parish culture than clarifying expectations, as important as this is. Those who are familiar with the research found in Growing an Engaged Church know that twelve factors have been identified that contribute to building a more engaged parish. We encourage you to study the book to learn more, and have included a Catholic study guide for it on the resource page for this workbook (link on page 84).

The engagement research helps us understand that people need to know what they get and what they give in order to be fully engaged in the parish. Knowing what is expected and that our spiritual needs will be met fall within the "what do I get" stage of becoming engaged. This question is deeper than "what's in it for me?" and is natural at the beginning stages of a relationship. One young adult workshop participant captured this when he shared, "Thank you so much for explaining that wondering what we 'will get' is natural. I was away from the Church for a while, and when I began to think about returning, I kept asking myself what the impact would be on me if I did so. It felt selfish at the time, but knew in my heart that if I was to join a parish I needed to know that it would make a difference in my life." Being able to offer our greatest talents and to contribute within the community is part of the "what do I give" stage of the process.[10]

---

[10] Growing an Engaged Church, 83

Pastoral leaders who have intentionally built engagement in their parishes over the last ten years witness to the fact that this is a process, with the ups and downs that are part of any systemic initiative. In Section Three, we will walk you through a process that includes identifying the expectations you hold for one another in your parish. As you will see, the process is crucial to the eventual acceptance and living out of the expectations in an ongoing way by parishioners. But clarifying expectations is only part of the process. Next, we will turn to the parish covenant as a means for communicating the expectations we hold within our parish, and more. The covenant places the process of intentionally building engagement in the context of our spiritual life with God and our life together in community.

At this time, use the worksheet below to guide your reflection on the information above, then continue to Section Two.

TAKE TIME TO EXPLORE TOGETHER. Use the worksheet below to guide your discussion. The worksheet masters are available in the participant guide, which is found via the link previously noted. Make a master copy of the worksheets to record your group's thoughts and insights for later use in planning. Use the space below to record additional insights or ideas for future reference.

CATHOLIC
LIFE & FAITH

Your Parish Relationships

BRIDGES
LEADERSHIP SERIES

What is the impact of clear expectations on your relationships?

How does your relationship with people in your parish have an impact on your faith?

Answer the questions below, then discuss with your group. Make a copy of this worksheet to compile group members' responses for future reflection.

Name a time in which having clear expectations in a relationship made a difference between yourself and another. What happened?	
What is the impact on your faith of being in relationship with others in your parish?	

What:
A Parish Covenant

What: A PARISH COVENANT

The parish is called to be a community of love that reflects the love of God and lives as the Body of Christ in the world. We are to be the living embodiment of Christ's self-giving love, nourished and sustained by Christ's very presence with us and for us, which we celebrate in the Eucharist. How do we draw parishioners more intentionally into this loving relationship? How do we encourage them to make it a driving force in their lives? As you might expect from the subtitle of this workbook, we believe this is best accomplished by a parish covenant through which parishioners regularly make a commitment to Christ and to your community. *A covenant is an intentional way to let parishioners know and fully understand all your parish offers to support them in their relationship with Jesus Christ, and the ways in which your parish hopes and expects that they will make a commitment to Christ and the community.* Notice the process involves two key elements: promises and commitments. We will explore both and why they are important in this section. The covenant is renewed regularly, inviting parishioners to examine the ways in which they have lived out commitments previously made, and encouraging growth in living discipleship over time.

WHY A COVENANT?

As we have shared this covenant process with parish leaders, the initial reaction of some has been to ask, "Why a covenant? Our covenant is with God." And yes, this is certainly so! A parish covenant is a means by which we invite one another to be a faith community that is an expression of our covenant relationship with God.

When we first hear the word "covenant," our ancestors in the faith come to mind: Noah, Abraham, and Moses. Their stories help us see God's constant, unfailing love, and our response, as we learn to live as God's people in the world. Throughout salvation history, God promises to love us. We make promises as well, and while humanity often fails to live our part of the covenant, Sacred Scripture attests to the witness of many holy men and women who responded to God's love with grace, fidelity, courage and strength. The communion of saints stand as witnesses, intercessors, and models who show us this holy life is possible in every age and stage of life, including our own time and place.

Jesus establishes the new covenant, a perfect expression of the love of God. He draws us into it as a way of living our daily lives. Every time we gather at Mass, we are drawn into Christ's sacrificial love. We hear him declare, "This is the chalice of my blood, the blood of the new and eternal covenant,"

> "At the heart of the new covenant is our realization that, in Christ, we are embraced by God's mercy and compassion and that our lives must bear witness to his love for all our brothers and sisters…Prepared for in the Old Testament and established by Christ in the fullness of time, the Church is a new people, founded on a new covenant… sealed with the blood of Jesus."
> Pope Francis, August 6, 2014

and we recognize that we, too, are called to offer ourselves for consecration, to be made holy, to be compelled to give of ourselves as Christ's people. We hear again and again, "Do this in memory of me," and we recognize that "this" is more than reception of Holy Communion. "This" is a way of life, of being members of Christ's body in the world, of sacrificing for the sake of others, giving glory to God.

Establishing a parish covenant is an expression and extension of this loving relationship between God and us. Not only does the covenant make clear what it means to belong to the parish, it actually clarifies the ways parishioners live out their covenant with God, and it helps us recognize that we need one another in order to live faithfully as Christian disciples. We are not a "me and Jesus" people, but rather are called to be in communion with Christ and with one another, "we" and Jesus!

LIVING IN COVENANT

The covenant of which many of us are most familiar is that of marriage. Whether we ourselves are married, we can grasp what living in covenant means by reflecting on this sacramental state of life. The couple, recognizing the love between them, promise to always be faithful to the other, to love the other no matter the circumstances that develop in their lives. Their love is a reflection of the love of God. It is a sacrament, a sign and bearer of God's grace. As we noted in the previous section, the spouses have expectations for one another. The marriage covenant calls the spouses to live for the other, to consider the spouse's needs before his or her own. Those who are married recognize the depth of commitment it takes to live in covenant love. It is a challenging and transforming way of life. When we think about marriage, it becomes easy for us to think about what a covenant entails.

WHAT DOES A COVENANT ENTAIL?

A covenant includes:

- An understanding of expectations
- Some sign or outward ritual (sacrifice, promise, practice)
    o   The things that will be accomplished as part of this relationship
- An agreement between the two parties
- An ongoing commitment
    o   This is what I give my highest priorities to
- A celebration, with a renewal of the promises made
    o   An annual celebration of the love and commitment that has been made

Establishing a parish covenant calls the people in the parish to make a commitment to Christ and to one another. Through the covenant process, parishioners are asked to take time to reflect on their relationship with God and with the community. In the covenant, the people acknowledge the promises the parish makes to them, and they make commitments to God and to one another, to grow in love and the way they live this love in their lives.

BUT WAIT!

Isn't the parish made up of the people who take part in the covenant? *Yes, exactly!* One of the many layers of recognition that comes to life through a covenant process is exactly this. *The people are the parish!* So when parish leaders and parishioners participate in a process through which they state what the parish promises to the people, they recognize the commitment that is necessary in order for the parish to be all it (they) are called to be. The parish is more than the priest, other clergy, staff and parishioner leaders, as important as all of these people are. The parish is the people, the body of Christ, the Church. So when "the parish" promises something, it is the people's participation that makes it so. Likewise, when the people make commitments to "the parish," they are committing to one another. God is present in both the promises and the commitments, and is made known as the promises and commitments are fulfilled, just as we encounter God's love in marriage when the spouses love one another through all of the circumstances of their lives. Establishing and living a parish covenant helps us to be open to a renewed encounter with God's love as we live out the promises and commitments of the covenant with one another.

In Section Three, we will walk through the development of the covenant, step-by-step. Take time now to reflect on the beauty of covenant love, using the worksheet below, then proceed to Section Three.

TAKE TIME TO EXPLORE TOGETHER. Use the worksheet below as your guide. The worksheet masters are available in the Participant participant guide, which is found via the link previously noted. Make a master copy of the worksheets to record your group's thoughts and insights for later use in planning. Use the space below to record additional insights or ideas for future reference.

The Joy of the Gospel

- Read this excerpt from The Joy of the Gospel.
- Underline or highlight words or phrases that strike you. Why is this important to you?
- Complete the question below and discuss your responses together.

"I invite all Christians, everywhere, at this very moment, to a renewed personal encounter with Jesus Christ, or at least an openness to letting him encounter them; I ask all of you to do this unfailingly each day. No one should think that this invitation is not meant for him or her, since 'no one is excluded from the joy brought by the Lord.'

The Lord does not disappoint those who take this risk; whenever we take a step toward Jesus, we come to realize he is already there, waiting for us with open arms. Now is the time to say to Jesus: 'Lord, I have let myself be deceived; in a thousand ways I have shunned your love, yet here I am once more, to renew my covenant with you. Save me once again, Lord, take me once more into your redeeming embrace.'"

(Evangelii Gaudium, 3)

What connections do you see between the renewal of the covenant of which Pope Francis speaks and the process of establishing a parish covenant which was discussed in this section?

How:
Six Steps to Creating a Parish Covenant

How: SIX STEPS TO CREATING A PARISH COVENANT

Deciding to create a parish covenant is a wonderful opportunity to identify and communicate the promises and commitments parishioners make to one another and to God. We would like to stress that this is not an overnight process. Based on our experience, it takes forming a dedicated team, a solid process, and the time and the involvement of the entire faith community to establish this practice that is both spiritual and practical.

Knowing the positive impact a covenant can have and the process that will be involved, there may be the temptation to jump ahead to the examples at the end of this workbook and just copy the text and change the parish name. At this point, it is important to stress that *THE PROCESS IS AS IMPORTANT AS THE OUTCOME.*

The reasons for this are three-fold...

- There is a direct correlation between involvement in the process and commitment of parishioners to the covenant. The more the parish is involved in this process the more committed people will be once the covenant is introduced.

- The process insures that parishioners will fully appreciate the reasons for the covenant and that it will be fully integrated into your parish's life and culture. When individuals feel that they are part of the establishment of the covenant, they are more apt to reinforce the visible impact it is has in their lives and the life of the community.

- The process insures that the covenant will be sustained. The more the covenant is reinforced year after year, the more it becomes part of the fabric of your parish. The annual renewal becomes something to which people look forward and new parishioners are introduced to the covenant by a parish that is committed to the process. Without these three elements, the covenant will be, at best, just another "flavor of the month" exercise and will die shortly after it's implemented. At worst, it will be met with skepticism, concern and defiance.

THE COVENANT PLANNING TEAM

Before you start this process it is important to identify your planning and implementation team that will drive the creation of your covenant. Some examples

- A subset of your existing pastoral leadership team, including your pastor and key staff
- A newly created covenant leadership team
- A selected representative group from your ministerial leaders
- *Please note, our suggestion is that this team be delegated authority for this initiative. They will be responsible for collecting data from the parties involved, distilling the information and developing the covenant. The process will insure that all input is taken into account, and having one group responsible will insure that the covenant preparation and implementation are enacted well.*

Once you have gathered your team, we suggest they spend the first meeting or two getting to know one another, perhaps working through the first workbook "Building Bridges to the Heart of Discipleship" and some of the exercises in it. In particular, they should discuss:

- What are our Hopes and Dreams for our parish?
- Why is a covenant important to our parish?
- How can a covenant can help meet our parish mission and vision, especially building committed disciples of Christ?
- Individual team members' talents and strengths

We also suggest that if possible the formation of the group includes team development, acknowledging the contribution each member can best make to the group. We strongly encourage the use of the StrengthsFinder assessment by Gallup. We've used this assessment in our own consulting with parishes specifically around forming teams and parish leaders with excellent results. You can access StrengthsFinder at www.gallupstrengthscenter.com. Workbook 3 of the Bridges Leadership Series will be an excellent resource for this if your parish is not already familiar with building strengths based ministry teams.

WORKING WITHIN YOUR ALREADY-EXISTING STRUCTURE

It is important to note that your covenant should fit into and reinforce any existing structure, developed vision/mission statement, and/or long range plan. Some parishes have spent extensive prayer and time discerning these sorts of elements, and insuring that the covenant is part of an already-existing framework insures consistency and sustainability. A worksheet is included at the end of this section to help you identify elements of your existing structure to consider in creating your covenant.

If you do not already have such structure, we propose a common and valuable framework for your consideration in Section Four.

THE SIX STEPS TO CREATING A PARISH COVENANT

The graphic below illustrates the six steps for creating a covenant.

They include identifying:

1) The parties involved in the covenant

2) The Promises your parish makes to each of your parishioners

3) The Commitments you ask of everyone who is a part of your parish

4) The length of your covenant and the renewal process

5) The sign and symbol of your covenant

6) The ritual that the parish holds to introduce and renew your covenant

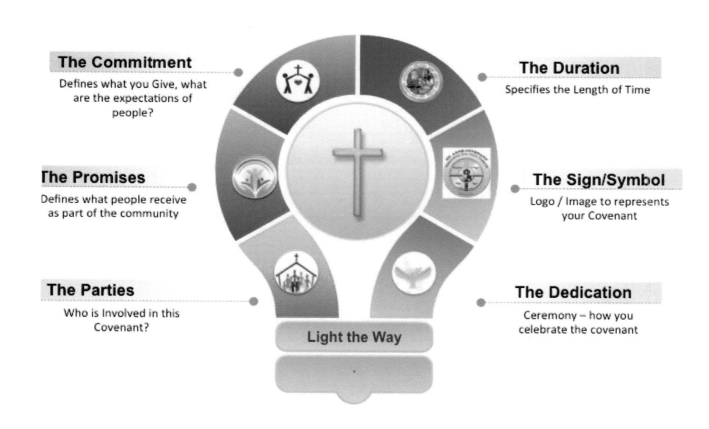

The Commitment
Defines what you Give, what are the expectations of people?

The Promises
Defines what people receive as part of the community

The Parties
Who is Involved in this Covenant?

The Duration
Specifies the Length of Time

The Sign/Symbol
Logo / Image to represents your Covenant

The Dedication
Ceremony – how you celebrate the covenant

Light the Way

The ultimate goal of the process is to provide clarity to each parishioner regarding what they get and what they give as members of the parish, laying the foundation for engaging them as disciples. Knowing that when they commit to the covenant, they are committing to live as good and faithful stewards and deepening their relationship to Jesus Christ.

Worksheets for Steps One, Two and Three are included at the end of this section. Your covenant team should become familiar with the process before beginning the worksheets.

STEP ONE: THE PARTIES

It is important to think about who is involved in the Covenant. Be as specific as possible. You will want to make sure your list is as complete as possible since these will be the parties you will be gathering feedback from.

STEP TWO: THE PROMISES

Promises are all things your faith community provides to each and every person who walks through your parish doors. This is important since no two parishes are alike. Each parish provides some similar and also different offerings. For instance, think about all of the weekend liturgies your parish offers: various Mass times, perhaps in more than one language, different styles of music, instrumentation, or musical leadership, sometimes with a rotation of presiders. Think about how your parish reaches out to the community such as Mobile Mall, Habitat for Humanity, Food Bank, etc. Think about your parish's ministry opportunities such as hospitality, liturgical, formation, social, etc.

What differentiates your parish from others? This is a great opportunity to reach out to your parishioners and get their input into what THEY see that your parish "promises". As one Pastor aptly put it, "Within a 25 mile radius there are 5 Catholic parishes. Sometimes it feels as if we are a drive-through; like any fast food chain, people come in, quickly look around, and if they don't like what they see they move on to the next one". Not all parishes have so many parishes from which people may choose, however, it is important to recognize that people do "size us up" as they experience our parishes. It is important to be clear about what your parish promises to it's parishioners. Otherwise they are left unclear and may miss the very ministry, offering or opportunity for service that they most need. If they don't see what they need or can't figure it out, they will quietly leave. This is why we believe Step Two in the process "Identifying Promises" is KEY. As one bishop said after one of our presentations, "You have given me a lot to think about in terms of what we truly promise our parishioners."

Ideas for gathering this information from your parish community:
- Invite your parish to attend a one-night listening group.
- Attend existing ministry meetings
- Attend your Pastoral Council meeting.
- Talk to your Pastor and staff
- Prepare a short questionnaire that you can give at the beginning of Mass to all your parishioners, send via email, place on the parish website, etc.

Sample interview questionnaires are included in the worksheets below. These can be modified to meet your parish's needs. The key is to create opportunities to listen to as many people as you can since this will 1) give you the perspective of the people who are part of your faith community and 2) create a higher degree of "buy-in" when you introduce the covenant to the community based on what they told you.

Factors that you may hear (hope to hear)…

✓ Great Liturgy	✓ Great Music
✓ Seminars/Retreats	✓ Bible Study
✓ Small Groups	✓ Welcoming environment
✓ Parish Functions	✓ Hospitality
✓ Pastor	✓ Outreach to the Community
✓ Adoration	✓ Prayer (Lectio Devina, Laybrinth)
✓ Life Teen	✓ Edge
✓ Alpha	

Are there themes that emerge as you listen?

After you've gathered the information…

As you reflect on each of the items, determine whether or not this item is something your parish consistently offers and can promise to your parishioners. Some items may be a one-time offering and not something that is the parish can promise on an ongoing basis. When you have distilled the information gathered, you are ready to draft the first part of the covenant which is to articulate all the promises you make as a faith community to those who come to your parish. Organize the promises you have determined into categories that correspond to your structure as indicated above (See the example from St. Anne's Church in Section Six for a wonderful illustration of this).

STEP THREE: THE COMMITMENTS

In this step you will define the expectations you have of your parishioners to fully participate in your parish community. Keep in mind, your goal is to lead to deeper sense of belonging within your community and ultimately deepen people's relationship with Christ.

As you look at all you offer, start a draft of the commitments you would like to see your parishioners make to God, to themselves and to your parish community. Again, it is helpful to organize the expectations in the same categories as the promises determined in Step Two.

STEP FOUR: THE DURATION

The process of introducing and renewing your covenant is critical. As you determine the timing and duration of your covenant make sure it is something that the parish can commit to and sustain over the years. Many parishes choose a specific weekend in the year and refer to it as "Covenant Weekend." As an example, for one parish, this occurs every first weekend in November and they have sustained this over the past six years.

Questions to ask:

- What time of the liturgical year makes the most sense to introduce our covenant?
- How can we insure that we introduce this as a renewable process?
- What ties can we make to other initiatives of our faith and/or parish life (for example, discipleship, stewardship, evangelization)?

STEP FIVE: SIGN OR SYMBOL

We often use symbols to represent an element or aspect of our faith. It is helpful to have some visual representation to communicate the meaning of your covenant. This visual representation is unique to each parish, as it is a sign of the particular character of your parish as well as the importance of your covenant and the place it takes in your parish community.

If you have graphic artists in your parish, this is a great opportunity to elicit their talents and gifts.

Once you've determined your symbol, consider the various ways it can be used to reinforce its significance. For instance:

- Magnets
- Cover of covenant handout
- Large banner in gathering space
- Bulletin Cover
- Website

STEP SIX: THE DEDICATION

Once you've determined the weekend of your covenant dedication, it is good to let people know it's coming a few weeks in advance. Let them know that there will be a dedication to your parish's covenant and use the weeks preceding the dedication as a time to explain

1) What is a covenant?

2) Why your parish is creating a covenant

3) The benefits to the community

4) Who was involved in creating the covenant

5) How the dedication will work

The Day of the Covenant Dedication

• Announcement at the Beginning of Mass

• Distribute a copy of the covenant at beginning of the homily or after the Communion rite

• Homily focused on covenant detail
• People sign the covenant and place in envelope

• Individuals then process to the sanctuary or designated place and put envelop into basket

** In some parishes, individuals include their name and address on front of sealed envelope. These commitment cards are then sent back a few weeks prior to the following year's dedication service with encouragement to reflect on previous commitments and to discern commitment for the coming year.

MAKE IT SYSTEMIC AND THEREFORE SUSTAINABLE

Once the covenant is clearly stated, the natural ties between the covenant and discipleship, stewardship and evangelization are easily captured and communicated. Making all of the connections possible, throughout the year, helps parishioners make ties to the covenant with the elements of parish life, and to remember their covenant commitments in their daily lives at home, work, school, parish and wider community. See the worksheets on pages 57-59 for a guided reflection on these systemic connections.

COMMUNICATE THE IMPACT OF THE COVENANT

Keep your covenant relevant, meaningful and sustainable by communicating the impact of the covenant on the parish community. This can be done through a letter sent to all parishioners, as an announcement at the end of Mass, as part of a homily or as a witness by those directly impacted. Making intentional connections between the ways in which parishioners are living the covenant and growth, service, or development of an engaging parish culture deepens the process over time, building bridges to the heart of the community.

TAKE TIME TO EXPLORE TOGETHER. Use the worksheets below as your discuss and plan. The worksheet masters are available in the participant guide, which is found via the link previously noted. Make a master copy of the worksheets to record your group's thoughts and insights for later use in planning. Use the space below to record additional insights or ideas for future reference.

Who are the parties involved in this Covenant?   (Pastor, staff, parishioners, children, ministry leaders, etc.) List everyone who will be impacted in the following space. Be specific. Consider your parish's current and potential future members.

Step Two: The Promises

Worksheet for Clergy, Staff, Councils and Leadership

What specifically do we offer people as members of our parish?

In what ways do we help parishioners grow spiritually?

In what ways do we help them live out their lives as disciples of Jesus Christ? How do we help them grow as good stewards?

Step Two: The Promises

Worksheet for the Parish Community

What originally brought you to our parish? What specifically has kept you here?

In what ways does our parish help you grow in relationship with God and to follow Jesus Christ?

In what ways does our parish help you grow as a disciple and a good steward?

CATHOLIC
LIFE & FAITH

Step Three: The Commitments

BRIDGES
LEADERSHIP SERIES

In what do we hope and expect every parishioner will participate in order to be open to an encounter or renewed encounter with Jesus Christ, to grow spiritually, or to grow as a person of faith?

What do we hope and expect every parishioner will do as people who love and serve the Lord, our community, and those in need?

Do you have a clear vision or mission statement? Is it simple enough that parishioners know it by heart?

Is there a clear parish structure through which all parish ministry and activity is organized? What are the key elements or categories of this structure? For example, Worship, Faith Formation, Stewardship, Community Life.

Do you have a current long range plan? If so, where in the life of the plan are you? If the plan is relatively new, what are the goal or objective areas, and do they correspond to structural elements/categories noted above?

If you answered "yes" to any of the questions above, list your primary elements or categories below. Organize your parish covenant by listing your promises and expectations in these categories.

Create Your Covenant Plan

BRIDGES
LEADERSHIP SERIES

Step	Who	By When
1: The Parties		
2: The Promises		
3: The Commitments		
4: The Duration		
5: Sign or Symbol		
6: Dedication		

How:
The Big Picture Comes to Life

How: BIG PICTURE COMING TO LIFE

It is always inspiring to visit a parish that has a clearly defined vision and mission statement, a positive leadership structure, and/or a manageable long range plan. Considerable prayer and time go into the discernment of such foundational elements of parish life. Many parishes are not there yet, for a variety of reasons. At times, the pastor is ready, but parishioner leaders need to be formed before taking on such endeavors. At other times, a pastor change, merger, cluster process or other major circumstance has taken precedence. Sometimes, an existing mission or vision statement is out of date, there is no discernible structure, or a long range plan has reached the end of its course.

Having an integrated parish structure is important, because without this, the many elements of parish life become like hangers without a closet. Everyone stays in their silo. Liturgical life is separate and apart from parish ministry, service and outreach; faith formation lacks a systemic tie to communal worship and the call to living discipleship. Not only this, parish ministries and organizations do not understand how each is part of the greater whole: groups vie for attention, funding, room allocation, and prominence. Having a "closet" (structure) in which each of the "hangers" hang (liturgical life, faith formation, ministry, service and outreach, for example) provides beneficial focus for everyone, creating a common vision, sense of mission and purpose, and understanding of how each contributes to the mission of the parish, fulfilling the mission of Christ in the world.

The parish covenant will naturally flow from an already-existing and still-living parish vision/mission, structure, and/or long range plan. Typically, such elements are manageable and clearly defined. If a structure is not already in existence or the current one is in need of updating, we would like to suggest what follows.

We appreciate the clarity and brevity of the framework we will share, as well as its biblical roots and connection to contemporary ecclesiology. In fact, we have noticed that many (we would go so far as to say most) of the parishes we have encountered that have an already existing structure mirror this framework to some degree. Other titles might be used for the characteristics named below, but the overall structure seems to be consistent. There are many good reasons for this, which we will share in what follows.

FOLLOWING THE EXAMPLE OF JESUS

As the early communities of believers were formed following Christ's ascension and the outpouring of the Holy Spirit at Pentecost, patterns of life and belief took shape, rooted in the experience of those who had walked with, learned from, and followed Jesus during his years of public ministry. They recalled their lives with Jesus and carried their experience to those who joined with them as disciples.

Jesus Worshiped: "…and as was his custom, Jesus entered the synagogue on the day of the Lord, and stood up to read." Luke 4:16

Jesus Connected: " There was a wedding at Cana in Galilee, and the mother of Jesus was there. Jesus and his disciples had likewise been invited to the celebration." John 2:1

Jesus Grew: "Jesus grew in wisdom and maturity and in favor with God and people." Luke 2:52

Jesus Served: "the Son of Man did not come to be served but to serve and give his life as a ransom for many." Matthew 20:28

WORSHIP, CONNECT, GROW AND SERVE: PARISH CULTURE CATALYSTS

As reflection on Jesus' life and ministry continued, these characteristics were consistently manifested. We see evidence of this in the Acts of the Apostles: "They devoted themselves to the apostles' *teaching (didache)* and *fellowship (koinonia)*, to the *breaking of bread and the prayers (leitourgia)*. Awe came upon everyone, because many wonders and signs were being done by the apostles. All who believed were together and had all things in common; they would sell their possessions and goods and distribute the proceeds to all, *as any had need* (diakonia). Day by day, as they spent much time together in the temple, they broke bread at home and ate their food with glad and generous hearts, praising God and having the goodwill of all the people. And day by day the Lord added to their number those who were being saved." Acts 2: 42-47 (italics and Greek words added) Through their living witness, they proclaimed Christ's saving life, death and resurrection (kerygma).

Leitourgia. Koinonia. Didache. Diakonia. Kerygma. These five characteristics have marked our Christian lives from the very beginning. As Christians, we **worship, connect, grow, and serve**, and through these actions, we proclaim Christ to all whom we touch with God's love.

These characteristics form a succinct and beneficial structure for parish life. Our parishes fulfill our mission to proclaim Christ and to form our members as Christian disciples when these characteristics mark our communal life as well as the lives of individual parishioners. They provide a framework for our ongoing spiritual growth. We can think of them as bridges, through which people enter into the Christian life more deeply, and through which the parish lives as the body of Christ. Not only this, over time, the culture of the parish is shaped by the deepening faith of its people who worship, connect, grow and serve. *We think of these four characteristics as culture catalysts.*

Scientifically, a catalyst is a spark that ignites action without itself being consumed. As Christian people, we rely on the spark of the Holy Spirit, enflaming our hearts, inspiring and strengthening our relationship with God as Christian disciples.

When we help one another to reflect on the ways in which we worship, connect, grow and serve, individually and within our parish, we ignite action in one another as missionary disciples. The parish culture becomes evangelizing: people are drawn to Christ, and ever more deeply to Christ, through the parish and its people. We will consider the role of the leader in forming and sustaining this culture at the end of this workbook, and will develop this in much greater depth in later workbooks in the Bridges Leadership Series.

The characteristics become a fitting means for organizing parish life, and our parish covenant. Note that we are using action verbs to describe the characteristics, and we focus on the four characteristics (worship, connect, grow and serve), understanding that we proclaim Christ through living and growing in these four ways.

If your parish does not already have a current organizational structure and/or pastoral plan, be attentive to these four characteristics as you develop in the future. Workbook 4 will provide a process for creating a parish structure and plan with these four characteristics as a framework.

If your parish has an existing vision/mission, organizational structure and/or pastoral plan, how do you see these four characteristics reflected in what is currently in place? Perhaps your parish uses words like prayer or spirituality for worship, for example; you might already have a group that focuses on faith formation or catechesis (grow); your parish may have a ministry that insures that service (serve) takes place, or a group that plans community events (connect).

Whether you already have a cohesive parish structure or need to develop one, recognizing these characteristics will help you categorize your promises and commitments for your parish covenant. Often the items you identified as promises or commitments will cluster around these four culture catalysts: Worship, Connect, Grow and Serve. Worksheets are found at the end of this section to organize your covenant through these four bridges.

How does your parish promise to provide ways for your parishioners to worship, connect grow and serve?

What commitments do you hope your parishioners will make to worship, connect, grow and serve?

REINFORCE THE COVENANT THROUGHOUT THE YEAR

A few parishes are using their parish structure to reinforce their covenant, strengthening parish leadership in the process. Each of ministries in a particular bridge (Worship, Connect, Grow, Serve) are assigned to two people on the Pastoral Council. Two people are assigned the "Worship" ministries, two are assigned the "Connect" ministries and so on. They are responsible for bringing those ministry leaders together twice a year as a way to connect all these leaders together. The goals and objectives of these meetings are to:

- Recognize and thank those leaders for the gift of their time and talent in leading their particular ministry
- Reinforce the specific ways that their ministries support the parish covenant
- Identify ways they can deepen and broaden the experience for their ministers of the four culture catalysts (additional ways we can worship together, grow together, connect and serve together")
- Identify ways that as a group (Worship, Connect, Grow and Serve) they can create for interdependent opportunities to support one another
- In what ways can the parish support their efforts

TAKE TIME TO EXPLORE TOGETHER. Use the worksheets below to guide discussion and planning. The worksheet masters are available in the participant guide, which is found via the link previously noted. Make a master copy of the worksheets to record your group's thoughts and insights for later use in planning. Use the space below to record additional insights or ideas for future reference.

CATHOLIC
LIFE & FAITH

Our Parish Promises
to Worship, Connect, Grow and Serve

BRIDGES
LEADERSHIP SERIES

WORSHIP	CONNECT	GROW	SERVE

CATHOLIC
LIFE & FAITH

Our Parishioners' Commitments
to Worship, Connect, Grow and Serve

BRIDGES
LEADERSHIP SERIES

WORSHIP	CONNECT	GROW	SERVE

Connect the Covenant with Discipleship

DISCIPLESHIP: Being a disciple is an ongoing process of following Jesus Christ with our lives. The path of discipleship is one of conversion, turning toward Christ, making conscious decisions to act as members of Christ's Body in the world.

In what ways does our covenant highlight the "promises and commitments" that will draw people to follow Jesus Christ with their lives?

Worship: In what specific ways does our worship draw people deeper in their relationship with Christ?

Connect: In what ways do we provide opportunities for people to share their faith with one another?

Grow: What formation opportunities do we offer to help people grow deeper in their knowledge and faith?

Serve: In what ways do we provide people the opportunity to serve others, as people who follow the example and command to serve given by Jesus?

Connect the Covenant with Stewardship

STEWARDSHIP: The call to live as good stewards leads us to recognize that all we are, have and will be are God's. Christian disciples grow in willingness to embrace Christ's self-giving way, which is the way of the steward. The steward recognizes that all is gift, grows in gratitude for the many blessings given and responds with generosity.

In what ways does our covenant highlight the "promises and commitments" for people to grow in gratitude and generously share their talents, gifts, time, and resources?

Worship: In what specific ways do we reinforce the message of stewardship in our worship practices?

Connect: In what ways do we provide opportunities for people to connect with others to share their stewardship practices or to be mentored by those who are living as good and faithful stewards?

Grow: What formation opportunities do we provide that help people discover and develop their God-given talents and gifts?

Serve: In what ways do we offer opportunities for people to use their talents, strengths and gifts within and outside our parish?

Connect the Covenant with Evangelization

EVANGELIZATION: We are called to share the Good News of Christ with others. Each of us needs to be evangelized, to be drawn more deeply to Christ, and that evangelization begins in our everyday interactions with others. We are called to live as missionary disciples, as people who evangelize through the ways in which we live our lives and share our faith with others.

In what ways does our covenant highlight the "promises and commitments" to support an evangelizing community?

Worship: As part of our worship, what specific ways do we reinforce our call to evangelize and bring the Good News to the world?

Connect: In what ways do we provide people the opportunity to share their witness stories?

Grow: In what ways do we form people to evangelize?

Serve: In what ways do we offer people the opportunity to share the Good News as part of our outreach activities?

Starting from Scratch:
The St. Anne Parish Story

Starting from Scratch: THE ST. ANNE PARISH STORY

St. Anne Parish in Byron, California was a small mission parish, founded almost one hundred years ago. With the arrival of a new pastor in the early 1990's, St. Anne started growing at a steady rate, requiring the building of a new Community Life Center to accommodate the new growth. Something that Fr. Ron Schmit, St. Anne pastor, wanted to maintain was the close community feel while the parish expanded. Upon reading the engagement research, Fr. Ron and a newly formed Engagement and Stewardship Council took on implementing a number of key initiatives rooted in the engagement research that would help maintain this close sense of community.

As they reflected on the need for clear expectations, they realized St. Anne already offered much to support people's spiritual growth. Through this reflection, their parish covenant was born. In total, their first covenant development process took over a year. With significant input from parishioners during the development phase, the covenant was received as an expression of the hopes, dreams and plans for the parish and its people as disciples and good stewards.

What you give to St. Anne

Many people do not realize it but each one of us is incredibly gifted. St. Paul tells us in the Letter to the Ephesians "We are God's creation, created in Christ Jesus to do good works, which God prepared in advance for us to do." Eph 2:10.

Our Covenant

As an active member of St. Anne Church I pledge to be partner in our mission to know Christ better and to make him better known I will:

Worship—to connect with Christ and God
- Attend weekly Sunday Mass to connect with God in the Body of Christ and frequently receive the sacraments
- Attend holy days
- Go to reconciliation at least once a year
- To be a person of prayer and spend at least 10 minutes a day in private prayer and or reading Scripture.
- Make Holy Week—Holy Thursday, Good Friday, Vigil of Easter, a spiritual priority and attend.
- Attend at least one other prayer opportunity—like monthly Eucharistic adoration or the ecumenical lessons and carols

Connect—our relationship with others
- Recognize Christ is in everyone and look for opportunities to meet others I do not know
- Look for opportunities to welcome new parishioners
- Participate in hospitality after Mass
- Attend at least one parish social function

Grow—to deepen our understanding of our faith
- Attend Family Faith Formation Class on Mondays with my family
- Attend one special lecture or read a book on faith or spirituality, subscribe to a Catholic magazine. Or join a small Christian Community

Serve—to imitate Jesus through acts of love.
- Spend at 1-2 hours a week in volunteering
- Join a ministry
- Volunteer time at special events and activities
- Look for opportunities to reach out to the community at St. Anne and at large
- To commit to contribute to my financial fair share for the operation of the parish-full share is $48 per week. I commit to a ___full share ___ half share ___quarter share ___other share $___

Stewardship—makes the covenant come alive!

November 16, 2008
COVENANT SUNDAY

ST. ANNE CATHOLIC CHURCH

ST. ANNE COVENANT
Stewardship:Time, Talent, Treasure

Worship Connect

St. Anne - Byron Catholic Community

Serve Grow

What You Get

What you Give

"TO KNOW CHRIST BETTER AND MAKE HIM BETTER KNOWN"

It took on implementing a number of key initiatives that would help main-

Our mission

We the members of St Anne community are called to:

- *Grow in the image of Christ through the Holy Spirit*
- *Be formed by the Word and our worship*
- *Use our gifts to welcome those who come and reach out to those who do not*
- *Take Jesus to the world of our daily lives*

Our Invitation to You

We invite you to join us as partners in the mission. Let us together get "to know Christ better and to make him better known. Partnership is the meaning of "covenant" God forms a covenant with us; and we with God. God equips us with gifts and strengths. Then invites us to use them collaborating with his loving plan. Won't you join us by entering into partnership/covenant with us?

Our Four Covenant Commitments

As partners in mission we commit together to use our gifts and strengths in four ways:

- **Worship**—to deepen our relationship with Christ and his Church, through prayer, mass and the sacraments.
- **Connect**—deepen our relationship with Christ's body, one another, by getting to know each other better
- **Grow**—to deepen our spiritual life, our faith and knowledge of Christ through learning and spiritual growth opportunities.
- **Serve**—to deepen the image of Jesus in us by imitating him who came "not to be served but to serve." To practice "acts of love."

What you get from St Anne

What we first and foremost **have to offer you is the God revealed to us in Jesus** and as he comes to us through his body, the Church. We pledge to offer him to you **through opportunities, open to all, to worship, connect, grow and serve.**

- **Worship**—each week we offer Sunday Eucharist, the center of our life together, to encounter Christ in each other in the word and all the sacraments. We offer Daily Eucharist, monthly Eucharistic Adoration and evening prayer; we celebrate quinceañeras, Taize Prayer and other opportunities for ecumenical prayer. We offer an annual celebration of the Passover Seder. We commit to making Holy Week the three days (Holy Thursday-Easter Sunday) of the Lord's passing from death to new life the center of our whole year. We commit to being people of personal prayer as well as people who pray together.

What you get from St Anne

What we first and foremost **have to offer you is the God revealed to us in Jesus** and as he comes to us through his body, the Church. We pledge to offer him to you **through opportunities, open to all, to worship, connect, grow and serve.**

- **Worship**—each week we offer Sunday Eucharist, the center of our life together, to encounter Christ in each other in the word and all the sacraments. We offer Daily Eucharist, monthly Eucharistic Adoration and evening prayer; we celebrate quinceañeras, Taize Prayer and other opportunities for ecumenical prayer. We offer an annual celebration of the Passover Seder. We commit to making Holy Week the three days (Holy Thursday-Easter Sunday) of the Lord's passing from death to new life the center of our whole year. We commit to being people of personal prayer as well as people who pray together.

- **Connect**—each year we offer many different opportunities for us to gather as a community and family. Some events are fundraisers, others are purely social so we can deepen in our love and care for each other. These are also good times for us to connect with the larger community beyond members of our parish. We pledge to reach out to each other especially those who are new to the community.

- **Grow**—there are many ways to deepen our faith and love of Christ at St. Anne. We offer the process for becoming Catholic--Rite of Christian Initiation for Adults (RCIA); Monday Family Faith Formation (K-adults), Preschool, Children's liturgy of the Word 10:30 Mass on Sundays (K-5ᵗʰ grade) teen ministry. Special lecture series, parish renewal (mission) and Small Christian Communities (faith sharing). We also offer the opportunity to discover your personal gifts through the "Strength Finder" instrument.

- **Serve**—There are many different opportunities to serve in the various ministries of St. Anne Church. These are listed in the ministry booklet or online. We pledge to continue to offer these opportunities and we affirm any service which you render outside of the parish community.

Stewardship—the energy that makes it all work

Stewardship is the recognition that all that I am and have is from God. It is a grateful acknowledgment of those gifts. It is the conscious decision to make a return in thanks

Link here to see the covenant on the St. Anne website:

http://stannechurchbyron.com/covenant/card.pdf

The covenant becomes the "closet in which all hangers hang":

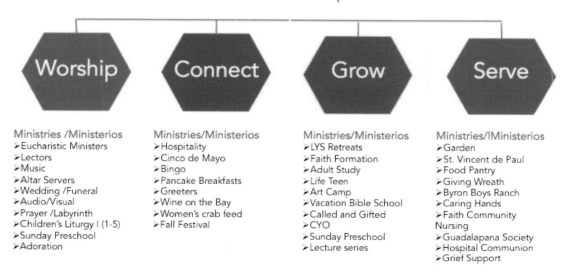

St. Anne Parish

Our Mission: We are a Christ-Centered Community Called to Worship, Connect, Grow and Serve

Our Vision: The Gospel

Worship

Ministries /Ministerios
- Eucharistic Ministers
- Lectors
- Music
- Altar Servers
- Wedding /Funeral
- Audio/Visual
- Prayer /Labyrinth
- Children's Liturgy I (1-5)
- Sunday Preschool
- Adoration

Connect

Ministries/Ministerios
- Hospitality
- Cinco de Mayo
- Bingo
- Pancake Breakfasts
- Greeters
- Wine on the Bay
- Women's crab feed
- Fall Festival

Grow

Ministries/Ministerios
- LYS Retreats
- Faith Formation
- Adult Study
- Life Teen
- Art Camp
- Vacation Bible School
- Called and Gifted
- CYO
- Sunday Preschool
- Lecture series

Serve

Ministries/IMinisterios
- Garden
- St. Vincent de Paul
- Food Pantry
- Giving Wreath
- Byron Boys Ranch
- Caring Hands
- Faith Community Nursing
- Guadalapana Society
- Hospital Communion
- Grief Support

AN EXAMPLE OF COVENANT COMMUNICATION

The following is a presentation made at the conclusion of the first year of the St. Anne covenant, in preparation for the second annual "Covenant Sunday." As you read this example, think about all the ways you might highlight all the great ways in which your parish can demonstrate the ways you Worship, Connect, Grow and Serve.

"Last November, Fr. Ron asked you to consider how you could be more engaged in the life of the parish. How we would become engaged in the church through worshipping, connecting, growing and serving. Fr. Ron asked us to sign our commitments and bring them to the altar. They have remained in this box, in front of the altar, all year, a gentle

reminder that we had promised God that we would be different, we would change, we would be involved. When you saw the statistics in the annual report, you had to conclude that God is engaging us to become the best that we can be. To be an engaged people. You saw the statistics, which were quite impressive. Now, let me tell you the rest of the story!

We WORSHIP. Our worship has grown. More people attend mass than ever before. People are coming from Brentwood, Antioch, Tracy, Mountain House, and one or two as far away as Walnut Creek (25 miles away). The growing cadre of altar servers enhance our Worship. Our Altar Server coordinator trains our altar servers. Some of these young people have been servers for more than five years. If you grew up when I did, it never occurred to anyone that families could join together to serve on the altar. Debbie helped change that perception by training young people and families to serve.

We are an engaged people.

Three years ago, a group of Spanish speaking people asked Fr. Ron to say Mass for the residents of a local trailer park. Attendance grew, and Mass moved to the rectory. Fr. Ron had to learn to read and speak Spanish, and the crowds overflowed. We were bulging at the seams. And Mass moved to the little church, and now to the large Community Life Center. Over 250 people make up a strong part of our parish ministry. They serve the entire parish with Cinco de Mayo celebrations, festivals Guadeloupe celebrations and rousing worship services. All of our parishioners are now brothers and sisters, comfortable with bilingual masses and other forms of worship. And Fr. Ron is currently in Bolivia, attending a Spanish immersion class.

We are an engaged people.

The Knights of Columbus, formed only four years ago, just received the Double Star Award from the Supreme Council. This is the highest award a council can receive, for supporting it's priest and for it's works of charity.

We are an engaged people.

We CONNECT. Thanks to the Hispanic Community, the Knights of Columbus, Women's Fellowship and others. Because of the efforts of these groups, this parish is connecting with each other and with the people in the wider community. We have had joint concerts with two other ecumenical churches in the area. We've hosted dinners with the ministers of the other churches. We have had great teen trips and people now stay longer for hospitality. Women's Fellowship sponsors 'Wine on the Bay' and 'Women's only Crabfeed'. The parish golf tournament attracts many who are not parishioners. Our small Christian communities meet twice a month to share the word and pray. This prayer gives the participants increased faith, unity and understanding. Their studies point out the relevance of the Word to their daily lives, to their need to serve and to connect.

We are an engaged people.

Our parish is made up of people who are active in their faith, know their fellow parishioners, serve the wider community and worship together in an uplifting spiritual setting.

We GROW. Jesus called us to grow in our faith and Matthew recorded it in the 28th chapter of his Gospel, sometimes called the Great Commission. Jesus urges us to 'go forth...make disciples of all nations, teaching them all I have commanded you.' The number of kids and adults in faith formation grows faster than we can keep up. Lower grade classes meet on Sunday morning, regular programs have expanded to two evenings during the week. Sr. Barbara joined our staff this year to lead our faith formation efforts. In the short time she has been here, there is a new energy, a new vibrancy to the program. Pre-K children are leading the prayers for all the age groups, seventh and eighth graders made over 300 fliers encouraging the use of Fair Trade Chocolate. They spend a Saturday morning, one week, making toys for abandoned pets.

The teen program brings God to a whole new generation of future leaders. One of the kids in the teen program, who family does not come to mass on Sunday, went to LA for the Religious Education Youth Conference. During the conference she turned to one of our leaders and said "I finally get it." The next Sunday, up and dressing for 8:30 Mass, the mom asked what was going on that early on a Sunday morning. The teen replied 'I am going to Mass: I want this feeling to continue.' How often do we, you and me, come back from a church experience and say, 'I get it'.

We are engaging people of all ages

We SERVE. The nursing ministry helped plan the setting up of an emergency Red Cross shelter and a disaster drill. They participate in Healing Masses. They held two blood drives and collected, enough blood to save 110 lives. They helped parishioners get the medical care they need and the community resources they need to life safe, comfortable lives.

We are an engaged people.

We began a parish garden ministry to help provide food for people in need. The need in the east county is so urgent, that the garden ministry is expanding the garden by 500 square feet. All summer long, vegetables were taken to St. Vincent de Paul and other churches for distribution to those who needed them. The garden ministry provided nearly 200 pounds of food each week to St. Vincent de Paul, who distributed it to people in need. The people who received the food lined the entry to Brentwood office and cheered the volunteers as they brought the food in. Now they are growing the winter crops because hunger doesn't take a vacation in the winter.

We are an engaged people.

Our CYO ministry set up a scholarship program for those who could not afford the registration fees. Some kids come from families with divorced parents, difficult home environments and many difficult situations. Many are served through CYO. It provides a structure they could not receive anywhere else.

We are an engaged people.

Parishioners have been going to the Boys Ranch for years, helping wherever they could, in addition to bringing the faith to these boys. One of our parishioners was eating at a nearby restaurant when a busboy approached and asked if he had been one of the adults who went to the ranch and the man answered 'yes.' The young man shared that he was recently released from the ranch and was now attending evening college and going to church every Sunday. He explained that until he had attended the weekly sessions with the volunteers from the parish, he had no idea that anyone cared about him. He certainly never thought Jesus loved him... He then hugged the man and said 'Thank you for giving me hope'.

We are an engaged people.

That's engagement.

The mission of our Diocese is 'To know Christ better and make Him better known'. We certainly contribute to that mission as we strive to meet our own parish mission.

The Gospel is our vision. This parish lives the Gospel and touches lives.

Our parish mission is to be a Christ Centered community called to Worship, Connect, Grow and Serve. This is what Christ asks us to do and to be. How can we say no? Next Sunday, we will take the opportunity to pray about our commitment to the mission. On November 5 & 6 we will celebrate Covenant Sunday. Once again, you will have the opportunity to discern and commit your support to our mission, and bring those commitments to the altar.

With the help of God, we will continue to be an engaged people."

THE KARLA RODRIGUEZ STORY — A TESTIMONIAL

Does a covenant really make a difference? Do people really take to heart the commitments they make as a result of the covenant? These were questions St. Anne's leaders asked when they first embarked down this path.

Karla Rodriguez is an eighteen year old active member of her parish. She participates in Life Teen, the choir and is a Youth Leader for Confirmation classes. One Sunday she asked her pastor if she could make an announcement during all the Masses about a ministry she wanted to begin. As Karla stood at the ambo, she began her announcement with the following statement. "I know here at St. Anne we are called to Worship, Connect, Grow and Serve. I have chosen to serve and I will be starting a blanket ministry for all the homeless in our area." She went on to explain the homeless situation in the surrounding area and asked parishioners to help by supplying blankets that she could then distribute to those in need. When asked later what inspired her, she shared that she felt compelled because of the reinforcement of the community to reach out to those who most need our help.

TAKE TIME TO EXPLORE TOGETHER. Use this space to record your reactions, ideas, and insights about the St. Anne experience and your parish's plans. Note the things you learned from reading about the St. Anne covenant, and connect to practices or strategies your parish may adopt as you create your parish covenant.

How: Discerning a Covenant within Stewardship Renewal

HOW: COVENANT WITHIN A STEWARDSHIP RENEWAL PROCESS

Many parishes have an established rhythm of annual stewardship renewal and commitment. Within this on-going process are elements such as lay witness talks, references to stewardship within the homily, articles in the parish bulletin, newsletter, and website, and faith formation for people of all ages. Most parish and diocesan stewardship processes include an annual time in which people are invited to reflect on their lives as disciples and stewards, consider how they are growing in gratitude and generosity, and make a renewed commitment to give of themselves, their time, talent, and treasure within all of the aspects of their lives, including their parish.

It is easy to see connections between stewardship renewal and a parish covenant. How are they different? Is there a way to include covenant language in an already-existing stewardship renewal process? How might a parish transition from stewardship renewal to an annual covenant? When is the best time to do so?

In many ways, parishes that have an annual stewardship renewal process are already clarifying expectations and inviting continued growth in commitment to Christ and to the parish. When stewardship is presented as a spiritual way of life, parishioners learn to appreciate their call to grow as disciples and stewards. In fact, teaching stewardship often focuses on our call: our call to grow in gratitude and generosity; to trust God in all things; to give of ourselves and our resources sacrificially, in recognition of the sacrificial, self-giving love of Jesus Christ.

While parishioners may recognize their call to give within an annual stewardship renewal process, they may not be consciously aware of the opportunities and expectations for growth in the whole of their lives as disciples and stewards, to worship, connect, grow and serve. One of the greatest benefits of the covenant process is that the promises and commitments we make to one another and to Christ are intentionally articulated and raised up as a vision for our lives as individuals and within the parish community.

DISCERNING A COVENANT

It is important to acknowledge that if your parishioners are responding to your current stewardship commitment process, transitioning to a covenant may not be advisable or necessary at present. Including covenant language may enhance your already-existing stewardship renewal by building on what is already working with your process. If your parish has hit a plateau, now might be the time to include covenant language as part of your stewardship commitment, or to transition to a covenant process. Use the worksheet at the end of this section to discern what is most appropriate for your parish at this time.

ADDING COVENANT LANGUAGE TO AN ALREADY-EXISTING RENEWAL

What might it "look like" to include an understanding of covenant within an already-existing stewardship renewal process? If your parish has an annual time in which you ask people to make a commitment to give of themselves and their resources, consider including connections to our covenant with God in Christ in your materials, lay witness talks, homilies, and/or bulletin articles. By doing so, you enrich your already-existing process, deepening the ways your parishioners are led to reflect on their lives as disciples and stewards. This might eventually lead to a transition to a more formal covenant, or you may arrive at a blended process that meets your needs.

At Immaculate Heart of Mary in Cincinnati, Ohio, simple adjustments were made to an already-existing process, with encouraging results. The annual stewardship process included materials specifically developed by the stewardship commission for that year. As the parish leaders learned about the importance of belonging and of clarifying expectations, the decision was made to include catechesis about our covenant relationship with God in Christ in the renewal materials. On the front cover was this letter from then-pastor, Fr. Jan Schmidt:

"Each year in the fall, we turn our attention to the ways in which we are following Jesus' call to love and serve as individuals and as a parish. In a special way this year, we remind ourselves of the covenant relationship we have with our God. No matter how far we may feel from god's presence, or what we may do to create distance between ourselves and our Lord, we are never abandoned nor beyond God's generous love. God's love never fails!

Our covenant with God calls us into covenant with one another, too. As members of the Body of Christ, each of us is needed to offer the gifts we have, a share of the many blessings we have received. the commitment you bring forward in the name of Jesus Christ on the weekend of September 29-30 will be a sign that you are growing as a steward and as a person made in the image of a giving God."

The commitment forms included a heading entitled "Our Covenant Commitment to God and Others: As a sign of my/our love of God and others, I/we commit to be good stewards in these ways in the coming year." The form included a line for the pastor's signature that read: "I sign this in recognition of your response to Christ's call as a disciple. In gratitude, [signature here]. The form was signed and photocopied, with the copy mailed to the family with a letter acknowledging and thanking the members for their commitment. They were invited to keep their commitment in a place in which all will be reminded of it.

The first year the parish adjusted their stewardship renewal process in these ways, commitment to ministry and financial giving significantly increased. Parishioners spoke of the new depth they recognized in their call to grow as stewards, and how their commitment is a sign of their love of God, and of their recognition of God's love in their lives. See samples of the materials described at www.CatholicLifeandFaith.net/samples.

THE BOTTOM LINE

Whether you start a covenant process from scratch, like St. Anne did, or you include covenant language to an already-existing stewardship renewal process, such as the example provided from Immaculate Heart of Mary, it is important to remember the reasons why we use such a process at all: to encourage and support people's spiritual growth by clarifying expectations, offering many ways in which people may grow and live as disciples, and by encouraging growth in all of the facets of our lives as we worship, connect, grow and serve. The process will necessarily arise from the experience and awareness of parish leaders who take into consideration current parish practice, and how the parish may grow as disciples and stewards in and for the future.

TAKE TIME TO EXPLORE TOGETHER. Use the worksheet below to guide discussion and planning. The worksheet masters are available in the participant guide, which is found via the link previously noted. Make a master copy of the worksheets to record your group's thoughts and insights for later use in planning. Use the space below to record additional insights or ideas for future reference.

Discerning a Covenant for Your Parish

Discover: Do you have an annual renewal process in which parishioners are encouraged to take a step in spiritual growth, expressed through stewardship of self, time, resources, talents and gifts? Do you see signs of growth through participation in Mass, communal prayer, increased ministry, outreach, or desire to serve? Do parishioners share the impact of their faith?

Has your parish hit a plateau in which the same people make similar commitments each year, with little increased participation or signs of spiritual growth among members?

Dream: Taking into account what you have read and discussed with the content of this workbook, what is your vision? How can you build bridges to the heart of your community through an annual time in which parishioners reflect on the promises made by the parish and in which they make a commitment to Christ and to the community?

Discern: How will you take a step from where you are to where you hope to be? If you parish does not have an annual time of discipleship renewal and commitment, how will you begin? If you already have a process in place, is it "working?" How might you enhance what is already in place in order to move toward your vision?

Do: Who will do what, how, in what timeframe?

The Covenant in Leadership Development

THE COVENANT IN LEADERSHIP DEVELOPMENT

Developing leaders is key to making the covenant sustainable in parish life and practice. Parish leaders need to not only own the covenant but also see themselves as the primary "bridge builders" of the covenant to those with whom they serve. As informal or formal leaders of the parish, you have responsibility for animating the ministry of others and for connecting those with whom you serve to the covenant and the greater mission of Christ in the world.

> "The Lord made bridges…Christians who are afraid to build bridges and prefer to build walls are Christians who are not sure of their faith, not sure of Jesus Christ…Build bridges and move forward."
>
> Pope Francis, May 8, 2013

Notice in the definition of the catalyst we previously shared that the catalyst is the spark that ignites action in others without itself being consumed. While the four catalysts of worship, connect, grow and serve spark action through the parish covenant, leaders contribute to the way the covenant is lived out by the ways in which they lead their groups and ministries in fulfilling the parish covenant, without themselves being consumed. Servant leadership is at its best when everyone is offered an opportunity to contribute, when people serve through their strengths, and when no one is overburdened by carrying too much responsibility and carrying it alone.

One option to increase this awareness and practice is to offer a day-long leadership development retreat that provides an opportunity to share your vision and goals and to emphasize the critical role parishioner leaders play in sustaining the focus and practice within the parish. Ultimately, this is a day for leaders to come together to share, reflect and plan ways in which to deepen the ties between the parish covenant and the ministers and parishioners in the parish. During such a retreat, leaders may be asked to discern the current ways they are modeling the integration and fulfillment of the covenant. In addition, this is a great opportunity to help leaders identify the ways they can help others grow in the area in which their ministry falls. Some examples of questions you may ask them to reflect on include:

Characteristic	Definition	Reflection Questions
WORSHIP	*Deepening our relationship to Christ and His Church through Prayer, Mass and the Sacraments.*	• In what ways do I "model" my belief in Jesus through my Worship practices? • In what ways have I been a "bridge" to others to our Worship Opportunities?
CONNECT	*Deepening our relationshiop with Christ's body, one another, by getting to know one another better.*	• How do I currently "connect" our community of ministers together? • How do I "bridge" opporutnities for fellowship, relationship and team building for those I lead?
GROW	*Deepeing our spiritual life, our faith and knowledge of Christ through learning and spiritual growth and opportunities*	• How do I currently "model" my own growth to others? • In what ways do I grow and develop the ministers I lead? • In what ways have I been a "bridge" for ongoing growth and development?
SERVE	*Deepening the image of Jesus in us by imitating Him who came "not to be served but to serve". To practice "acts of love".*	• In what ways do I "model" serving in our community and beyond? • In what ways am I a "bridge" to my ministers and opportunities to serve?

YOUR NEXT STEPS

As we conclude this second module of the Bridges series, identify your immediate next steps:

- Schedule a meeting. If you have formed a Covenant team, give that group time to gather input and develop an initial list of your parish's promises and commitments. When they are ready, schedule a meeting with all who will be involved in finalizing the covenant and who will bring it to your parish community;

- Develop an initial plan for introducing the covenant to your parish, and for implementing it for the first year;

- Discuss ways in which your parish leaders should be involved in implementing the covenant process;

- Be attentive to the ways in which people express growth in discipleship as a result of living your covenant.

- Consider which elements of the Bridges path are appropriate for your parish. See description of the path and the resources to help you on this journey, beginning on page 74;

- Determine what group(s) will continue with the Bridges series module 3 on Building Strengths Based Ministry Teams;

- Continue to explore through the web series Bridges Now, and consider a live or virtual session for your leaders with one of the Catholic Life and Faith team. Contact us via the link on the Bridges website: www.Bridge2Faith.net.

- Please take our brief survey about this workbook and the Bridges Leadership Series. Your feedback, experience, and insights will enhance the ways we may partner with leaders like you in the future. The survey is here: https://www.surveymonkey.com/s/BridgesBook

You have taken a big step toward an engaging and evangelizing community through the discussions and plans you have made as you have progressed through this workbook! Just as we are never "finished" disciples, so too, our communities are never "finished." As soon as we begin to think that we are, we either continue to build and to grow, or we become complacent and stagnant.

The Bridges path takes this need for continual growth and deepening in faith and practice into account and provides a structure for the ongoing development of the faith community. In what follows, we highlight the steps on the path, and share with you the ways in which Catholic Life and Faith is ready to help you, as your partners in ministry.

THE BRIDGES PATH

Form servant leaders as bridge builders who:

Step One: Hold a common vision of the engaging and evangelizing community and who grasp the importance of building bridges to others within the community and beyond it;

Step Two: Deepen community by clarifying expectations and establishing a parish covenant through which parishioners are engaged as people who worship, connect, grow and serve;

Step Three: Build talents into strengths, develop strengths based ministry teams, and create a parish climate in which every person has the opportunity to contribute his or her best within the community;

Step Four: Lead and participate in guiding groups that carry the vision of an engaging and evangelizing community forward. These teams provide on-going input for initiatives in the four key areas of parish life (worship, connect, grow and serve) and take responsibility for building and strengthening bridges among parishioners through their area of influence and responsibility.

THE BRIDGES PATH

Develop a common vision of and begin to build an
engaging and evangelizing community
Form your leaders (see resource list below)

Then:
Form four guiding teams

Worship	Connect	Grow	Serve
Mass, Sacraments, Liturgical Ministry Formation	Communal life, Welcome, Friendship	Call to Discipleship, Faith Formation for All	Call to Live as Stewards, Sharing of Self, Resources, Faith
Take stock of current of liturgical and sacramental practices	Take stock of current communal practices	Take stock of current discipleship and faith formation practices	Take stock of current stewardship, service, and outreach practices
Develop a plan to enhance the celebration of the liturgy and the ways people are formed for full, conscious and active participation	Develop and implement a parish covenant Enhance welcoming Create opportunities for friendship Connect team coordinates on-going development of community	Develop a comprehensive plan for faith formation-for-all 6 tasks of catechesis One size does not fit all	Develop a plan to form people as good stewards Strengths for individuals, in ministry teams; Strengths-based approach permeates parish Regular call to service, justice, mercy, ministry
On-going development via Worship team	On-going development via Connect team	On-going development via Grow team	On-going development via Serve team

Quarterly meeting of leaders
Annual retreat and renewal for leaders and for all
Skill development for servant leaders

HOW CATHOLIC LIFE AND FAITH IS READY TO PARTNER WITH YOU

Live and Virtual Events
Workbooks with Learning Videos and Guides
Parish Consulting and Partnership

The Bridges Series Servant Leader Workbooks:

Building Bridges to the Heart of Discipleship:
Three Initial Steps to an Engaging and Evangelizing Community

Building Bridges to the Heart of the Community:
Six Steps to Creating a Parish Covenant

Building Bridges to the Heart of Your People:
Discovering and Living Strengths for an Engaging Parish Culture

Building Bridges to the Heart of the Parish:
Culture Catalysts in Parish Structure and Planning

Worship: Building Bridges to the Heart of the Liturgy

Connect: Building Bridges to the Heart of One Another

Grow: Building Bridges to the Heart of Our Faith

Serve: Building Bridges to the Heart of the Steward

LEARNING VIDEO AND GUIDE

The accompanying learning video and guide is found here at the link here:

www.Bridge2Faith.net/workbook2

Your password is: Bridges2 (password is cap sensitive)

The materials include:

1. A learning video which introduces the theological foundation for the covenant
2. A participant guide that accompanies this workbook and includes all worksheet masters
3. An optional introduction to engagement video

Made in the USA
Charleston, SC
24 September 2015